*Children learn to read by **reading**, but they need help to begin.*

When you have read the story on the left-hand pages aloud to the child, go back to the beginning of the book and look at the pictures together.

Encourage children to read the sentences under the pictures. If they don't know a word, give them a chance to "guess" what it is from the illustrations before telling them.

There are more suggestions for helping children learn to read in the *Parent/Teacher Guide*.

LADYBIRD BOOKS, INC.
Lewiston, Maine 04240 U.S.A.
© Text and layout SHEILA McCULLAGH MCMLXXXVI
© In publication LADYBIRD BOOKS LTD MCMLXXXVI
Loughborough, Leicestershire, England

Printed in England

The Magician's Party

written by SHEILA McCULLAGH
illustrated by GAVIN ROWE

This book belongs to:

Ladybird Books

It was November, but it wasn't very cold.
Davy and Sarah were sitting on the steps
of their house in Puddle Lane.

"Do you remember this time last year?"
asked Sarah. "We had a party, and
everyone came."

"I wish we could have a party this year,"
said Davy.
Sarah stood up suddenly.
"We can!" she said.
"We can have a party out here,
in Puddle Lane."

Sarah stood up.

"Let's get Pedro and Rosa,"
said Davy. "I'm sure they'll help."

They were just starting down the lane,
when Pedro came out of his house.

"We're going to have a party, Pedro,"
said Sarah. "We're going to have it
out here, in the lane."

"Rosa and I could bring some lemonade,"
said Pedro.

Davy and Sarah
met Pedro
in Puddle Lane.

Miss Baker came up the lane.
"You're looking very excited,"
she said. "Has something happened?"

"It hasn't happened yet,
but it's going to," said Sarah.
"We're going to have a party
in Puddle Lane."

"What a good idea!" said Miss Baker.
"I'll bake some cookies for you."

Miss Baker
came up Puddle Lane.

Just then, Mr. Gotobed
came out of his house.
"What's happening?" he asked.
"We're going to have a party
in Puddle Lane," said Sarah.
"Will you come, Mr. Gotobed?"
asked Davy.

"Of course I will," said Mr. Gotobed.
"I have a table you can use, too."

Mr. Gotobed
came out of his house.

Miss Baker had gone off to start baking.
Mr. Gotobed was just about to go back
into his house,
when Peter Puffle came up the lane.

"What are you doing?" he asked.

"We're going to have a party,"
said Davy. "Would you like to come?"

Peter Puffle
came up the lane.

"My Grandpa took me to a party
last summer," said Peter.
"There were fireworks!
Are you going to have fireworks?"

"No," said Sarah.

"It won't be much of a party
without fireworks," said Peter.
"**I'm** not coming."

"Are you having fireworks?"
asked Peter.

Peter went back down the lane,
blowing his horn.
Sarah and Davy and Pedro
looked very unhappy.

Peter went back
down the lane.

"Don't mind him,"
said Mr. Gotobed.
"You don't need fireworks
to have a party.
All you need are cheerful people.
You get the things ready,
and we'll have that party."

"Don't mind Peter,"
said Mr. Gotobed.
"We will have that party
in Puddle Lane!"

Mrs. Pitter-Patter came up the lane.
"What are you talking about?"
she demanded.

"We're going to have a party
in Puddle Lane," said Sarah.

"I hate noisy parties,"
said Mrs. Pitter-Patter.
"Didn't I hear Peter Puffle
say something about fireworks?
You're not going to
have fireworks, are you?"

"No," said Sarah.

"I'm very glad to hear it,"
said Mrs. Pitter-Patter.
She went back down
the lane.

"I wish we **were** going to
have fireworks," said Davy.

"You are not
going to have fireworks,
are you?"
asked Mrs. Pitter-Patter.

The Magician lived in the house
at the end of Puddle Lane.
He had been out in his garden.
Nobody had seen him, but
he had heard every word.
"I think **I'll** go to this party,"
the Magician said to himself.
"Then there **will** be some fireworks!
But I'll tell the Griffle first."

The Magician was
in his garden.
"I will go to the party,"
he said.

The Griffle lived in
the Magician's garden.
He could vanish when
he wanted to, and
he was shy and nervous.
He appeared as soon as
the Magician called.
"Griffle," said the Magician,
"I wanted to warn you.
There's going to be a party
in Puddle Lane tonight.
I'm going to make some magic fireworks."

The Magician called the Griffle.
The Griffle came.
''I am going to make
some magic fireworks,''
said the Magician.

"I don't like fireworks,"
said the Griffle.
He looked very unhappy.
"I know you don't,"
said the Magician.
"None of the animals in the garden
like fireworks. They're scared
of all the flashes and bangs.
I want you to tell them
to stay home and hide.
Then they won't be frightened."

"I think I'll hide myself,"
said the Griffle.

"You can hide in my room,"
said the Magician. "But
tell the other animals first."

"I don't like fireworks,"
said the Griffle.

So the Griffle went around
to the other animals in the garden,
and warned them to stay
inside for the evening.
He left a note in the old tree
for the mice. (The Griffle
was afraid of mice, and
he didn't want to see them.
But he knew that Grandfather Mouse
had learned to read, when he lived
in Mr. Wideawake's toy store.)

The Griffle left a note
for the mice.
He left it
in the old tree.

In Puddle Lane, everyone
was getting ready for the party.
Mr. Gotobed opened his door, and
called Davy to help him.
Between them, they carried a table
out into the lane.
Soon Miss Baker
came out of her house
with a big tray of cookies.
Pedro ran home,
and came back with Rosa,
and a big pitcher of lemonade.

Pedro ran home.
He came back with Rosa.

They were just about to begin,
when they heard music.
Someone was singing in Puddle Lane.
They couldn't see anyone, but
they could hear the words clearly:

There's magic in the air.
There's magic all around.
There's magic in the sunshine.
There's magic in the ground.
There's magic in the puddles.
There's magic in the rain,
when you belong to Candletown,
and live in Puddle Lane.

Someone was singing
in Puddle Lane.

The gates at the end of the lane
opened, and the Magician came through.
"I thought you might like
some fireworks," he said.

"Fireworks!" cried Sarah and Davy.

"Fireworks!" cried Pedro and Rosa.

"Yes, fireworks," said the Magician.
"Watch!"
And he snapped his fingers.

The Magician
came into the lane.
''Fireworks!'' said the Magician.
And he snapped his fingers.

At once, the fireworks began.
There were red and green stars,
and whirls of fire.
There were loud bangs.
There were blue and yellow stars,
and flashes of light.

The fireworks began.
There were red and green stars.
There were blue and yellow stars.

Mrs. Pitter-Patter came rushing
up the lane.
"What on earth are you doing?" she cried.
"You said you weren't having fireworks!"

"Are you afraid of fireworks?"
asked the Magician.
"Of course not!" snapped Mrs. Pitter-Patter.

"Then you won't mind a few, will you?"
said the Magician.
"I'm making some magic fireworks tonight."

A firecracker went off in the lane.
"Stop it!" cried Mrs. Pitter-Patter.

"You go home," said the Magician.

Mrs. Pitter-Patter
came up the lane.
"You go home,"
said the Magician.

Mrs. Pitter-Patter was very angry.
She was just about to say
that she wouldn't go home,
when she remembered that this
was a very great magician.
She tossed her head, and
went down the lane.
When she got to her house,
she went inside, and slammed the door.
The Magician laughed.
He snapped his fingers, and
rockets shot up into the sky.

The Magician
snapped his fingers.

When at last the fireworks were over,
they had the cookies and lemonade.
Sarah and Davy's mother
came out to join them,
with a big cake she had baked.

"It's the best party
we've ever had!" said Davy.

When the fireworks were over,
they had a party
in Puddle Lane.

Notes for the parent/teacher

Turn back to the beginning, and print the child's name in the space on the title page, using ordinary, not capital letters.

Now go through the book again. Look at each picture and talk about it. Point to the caption below, and read it aloud yourself.

Run your finger under the words as you read, so that the child learns that reading goes from left to right.

Encourage the child to read the words under the illustrations. Don't rush in with the word before he/she has had time to think, but don't leave him/her struggling.

Read this story as often as the child likes hearing it. The more opportunities he/she has to look at the illustrations and **read** the captions with you, the more he/she will come to recognize the words.

If you have several books, let the child choose which story he/she would like.

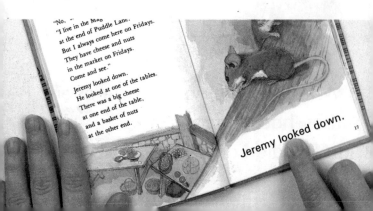